# The Midnight Breakout

Sunny V.

Published by Sunny V., 2025.

THE MIDNIGHT BREAKOUT

**First edition. December 16, 2025.**



ISBN: 979-8233650567

Written by Sunny V..

# DISCLAIMER

## Read This Before You Turn the Page

**This book is not financial advice. It is financial philosophy.**

The content within *"The Midnight Breakout"* is for educational and entertainment purposes only. The author is not a Registered Investment Advisor (RIA), a Certified Public Accountant (CPA), or an Attorney.

This book explores high-risk strategies, including but not limited to: asymmetric speculation, cryptocurrency trading, the use of leverage/ debt, and aggressive tax planning.

**By reading this book, you acknowledge and agree to the following:**

1. **No Fiduciary Relationship:** No client-professional relationship is established by your use of this book. The strategies mentioned are generalizations and do not take into account your specific financial situation, risk tolerance, or local laws.
2. **Risk of Ruin:** The concepts of "Hyper-Speed Wealth" inherently involve **high volatility and high risk**. While the upside is uncapped, the downside can be total. You should never invest money you cannot afford to lose.
3. **Do Your Own Research (DYOR):** You are responsible for your own due diligence. Before executing any strategy, especially those involving tax law (Chapter 17) or asset protection (Chapter 16), you must consult with your own qualified legal and tax professionals.
4. **No Guarantees:** Past performance is not indicative of future results. The financial markets are unpredictable. What worked yesterday may not work tomorrow. The author and publisher assume no responsibility or liability for any errors or omissions

in the content of this book, nor for any losses or damages that may result from the use of the information contained herein.

**The "Turtle" takes no risks and gets no rewards. The "Sniper" takes calculated risks but understands the consequences.**

You are the captain of your own ship. If you steer it into a storm based on what you read here, you are responsible for steering it out. **Proceed at your own risk.**

# INTRODUCTION

## The Great Deception

If you picked up this book hoping for a comforting guide on how to save five dollars a day, cut back on lattes, and retire with dignity at the age of sixty-five, I have a piece of advice for you:

**Put this book down. Immediately.**

Go buy a mutual fund brochure. Go listen to the financial gurus who smile on morning television and tell you that "slow and steady wins the race." Go back to the herd.

This book is not for people who want to get rich *eventually*.

This book is for people who want to get rich *now*.

I am writing this because you have been the victim of a heist. You haven't been robbed of your money; you have been robbed of something far more valuable. You have been robbed of your **Time**.

For generations, society has peddled a toxic script called "The 40-Year Plan." It goes like this: Go to school. Get a safe job. Rent out your time five days a week. Save 10% of your paycheck. Invest in a diversified portfolio that yields 7% a year. Wait. Wait. Wait.

And then, if the economy doesn't collapse, and if you don't get sick, and if inflation doesn't eat your savings, you can wake up at age 65 as a millionaire.

Congratulations. You are now the wealthiest person in the geriatric ward. You have the money to buy a Ferrari, but your back hurts too much to get into the seat. You have the time to travel the world, but your energy is gone.

That is not wealth. That is a consolation prize for a life spent in servitude.

**Wealth without youth is a trap. Wealth without time is useless.**

If you want to be free while you still have the vitality to enjoy it, you cannot take the Slow Lane. You cannot rely on compound interest. You cannot trade your time for money.

You need to understand the **Physics of the Breakout.**

Look around you. The rules have changed. The industrial age is dead. The digital age has rewritten the laws of cause and effect.

We see twenty-year-olds becoming multi-millionaires in six months.

We see solo founders building billion-dollar companies with zero employees.

We see crypto wallets exploding from three figures to seven figures overnight.

The world looks at these events and screams, "Luck!" "Gambling!" "Anomaly!"

They are wrong.

These are not anomalies. They are the result of **Asymmetry**. They are the result of specific, replicable mechanics that allow wealth to be compressed, not accumulated.

This is the science of **Hyper-Speed Wealth**.

This book is about rejecting the linear equation of "Time = Money."

It is about disconnecting your income from the clock.

It is about building systems, assets, and leverage that work 24 hours a day, 365 days a year, with zero marginal cost.

We are going to explore the dark arts of the new economy. We will talk about:

- **The Velocity Mindset:** Rewiring your brain to hunt for exponential returns.
- **The Vehicles:** Using code, media, and volatility to move faster than the market.
- **The Setup:** How to position yourself so that when luck strikes, it strikes hard.
- **The Morning After:** How to keep the money once the

floodgates open.

I will warn you: The concepts in this book are aggressive. They are risky. They require you to kill the "employee" inside of you. They require you to stop acting like a tortoise and start thinking like a predator.

The premise of this book is simple:

**You do not need 40 years to get rich.**

You need 3 to 5 years of intense, focused, asymmetric warfare, followed by a single event that changes your life overnight.

We call this event **The Midnight Breakout.**

The clock is ticking. You are dying a little bit every minute you stay in the slow lane.

Let's speed up.

# Chapter 1: The Turtle Dies

**Why Slow and Steady is a Death Sentence**

You were lied to before you even learned to read.

It started with a children's book. You know the one. A smug, hyper-active hare races a plodding, disciplined tortoise. The hare is talented but arrogant; he sprints, gets tired, and takes a nap. The tortoise, embodying the virtues of the industrial worker, head down, slow pace, never complaining, keeps walking.

The tortoise crosses the finish line. The hare loses. The moral is branded into your psyche: Slow and steady wins the race.

In the real world, the tortoise doesn't win. In the real world, the tortoise gets run over by a semi-truck on the interstate. Or, more accurately, the tortoise starves to death because by the time he reaches the lettuce, it has already rotted.

The "Slow and Steady" doctrine is not a roadmap to wealth; it is a prescription for mediocrity and a comfortable sedative for the working poor. It is a fairy tale told by the wealthy to the workforce to keep them showing up on Monday morning.

If you want to become a millionaire overnight, or fast enough that it feels like overnight, the first thing you must do is kill the turtle.

*"I remember the exact moment the "Turtle" died inside of me. It was a Tuesday in November. I was twenty-five years old.*

*I was sitting in a grey fabric cubicle under humming fluorescent lights that gave everyone in the office a sickly, yellow tint. I was working on a spreadsheet for a boss who didn't even know my last name.*

*I had done everything right. I got the degree. I got the job. I packed my lunch to save money. But that afternoon, a cold realization hit me: I have been doing this for three years, and I have forty more to go.*

*I pulled up a compound interest calculator on my second monitor, hiding it so my manager wouldn't see. I punched in my numbers. I entered my salary. I entered my pathetic savings rate. I hit "Calculate" to see when I would finally be free.*

*The screen blinked back at me:* ***Age 68.***

*I felt a physical wave of nausea. I looked around the office at the older guys, heads down, spines curved, eyes glazed over, and realized I wasn't looking at my colleagues. I was looking at my future. I was trading the absolute prime of my life for a "maybe" at the very end of it.*

*I walked out to the parking lot, sat on a bench, and thought to my-self for a while.*

*That was the day I stopped listening to the advice of average people. That was the day I realized that playing it safe was the most dangerous thing I could possibly do."*

**The Math of the "Slow Lane"**

Let's look at the "Get Rich Slow" plan pushed by every financial guru on morning television. They smile with bleached teeth and tell you the secret to wealth is skipping your $5 latte, saving 10% of your paycheck, and putting it into a diversified index fund.

They call this "The Miracle of Compound Interest."

Let's run the math on their miracle.

Assume you earn $60,000 a year. You are disciplined. You suffer. You pinch pennies. You manage to save a net $6,000 a year (10%). You dump it into the stock market, which historically returns about 7% per year (adjusted for inflation, if you're lucky).

Do you know how long it takes that $6,000 annual investment to turn into $1 million?

**40 years.**

If you start at age 25, you will be a millionaire by age 65.

Congratulations. You are now the wealthiest person in the nursing home. You have a million dollars, but you also have arthritis, failing eyesight, and a bladder that won't cooperate. You traded your prime years, your energy, your libido, your ability to experience the world, for a safety net at the very end of your life.

That isn't wealth. That is a consolation prize for a life unlived.

**The Inflation Shark**

The situation is actually worse than the math above suggests. The "Slow and Steady" strategy assumes the road is flat. It isn't. You are running on a treadmill that is speeding up.

This treadmill is called **Inflation.**

Real inflation is rarely the "2%" the government claims. Real inflation is the cost of housing, education, healthcare, and assets. While you are diligently saving your 10%, the cost of buying the "Freedom" you want is rising by 5%, 10%, or 20%.

If your savings rate is linear (slow) and asset inflation is exponential (fast), you are technically becoming poorer every day you save.

The Turtle is walking forward at 1 MPH, but the ground beneath him is moving backward at 5 MPH.

**Wealth is a Function of Velocity**

To break out of the gravitational pull of the working class, you cannot rely on *Time*. You must rely on *Velocity*.

Wealth is not created by accumulating scraps over decades. Wealth is created by **events.**

- Zuckerberg didn't save 10% of his paycheck to get rich. He created an event (Facebook IPO).
- Cuban didn't skip lattes. He created an event (Selling Broadcast.com).
- The crypto-kid down the street didn't wait 40 years. He caught a velocity spike (an Event).

"But those are outliers!" you scream. "I'm not Zuckerberg!"

You don't have to be. You just have to understand the physics of money. Money likes speed. Money likes leverage. Money flows to where value is created *quickly* and *massively*.

The "Overnight Success" is not a myth. It is simply a misunderstanding of physics. An explosion looks instantaneous to the observer, but it is the result of pressure, chemical mixture, and a spark.

This book is about how to mix the chemicals and light the fuse.

**Speed is Safety**

The biggest lie of the "Turtle" mindset is that going slow is safer.

"Don't take risks," they say. "Keep your steady job."

Is it safe to have one income stream that can be turned off by a grumpy boss or a generic AI algorithm on a Tuesday morning?

Is it safe to rely on a pension fund managed by people who don't know you?

Is it safe to bet 40 years of your life that the economy won't collapse right before you retire?

No. That is the highest risk gamble imaginable.

**Speed is safety.**

When you make money fast, you remove the variable of time. If you make $1 million in 12 months rather than 40 years, you have eliminated 39 years of risk. You have beaten the market. You have beaten inflation. You have secured your freedom while you are still young enough to use it.

**The Shift**

From this page forward, we are done with the turtle. We are done with "sensible" advice for average people. If you want average results, go read a different book.

We are here to hunt the Black Swan. We are here to engineer luck.

We are going to rewire your brain to stop looking for "steady returns" and start looking for **Asymmetric Bets**, opportunities where the risk is low, but the potential reward is explosive.

You are not going to crawl to the finish line. You are going to build a rocket, strap yourself in, and light the fuse.

It might blow up on the launchpad. That is a risk.

But the alternative is walking for 40 years only to find out the finish line was moved.

Let's get moving.

# Chapter 2: The Law of Asymmetry

## The Math of Getting Rich Quick

Most people stay poor because they are bad at math.

I don't mean calculus or trigonometry. I mean the basic probability mechanics of life.

The average person structures their entire existence around **Linear Risk**. They trade X hours for Y dollars. They seek "steady" returns. They equate stability with safety. In the casino of life, they are betting on Red or Black. They put a dollar down to win a dollar back.

If you want to become a millionaire overnight, you have to stop betting on Red. You have to stop looking for 1:1 returns.

You need to find the bets where you put $1 down to win $10,000, but, and this is the key, if you lose, you only lose that single dollar.

This is the **Law of Asymmetry**.

It is the only mathematical formula that allows wealth to be compressed into a short timeframe. If you ignore this chapter, the rest of the book is useless. You cannot hyper-scale a linear equation.

## The Trap of Symmetry (Linear Hell)

Let's look at your day job.

You work 40 hours. You get paid for 40 hours.

If you work really hard, maybe you get a 5% raise.

If you get sick and can't work, you get paid zero.

This is a **Symmetrical/Linear Trade**. The input matches the output.

The problem with symmetry is that it has a **Capped Upside**. There are only 24 hours in a day. Even if you are a high-paid lawyer billing $1,000 an hour, you are still capped. You cannot become a billionaire billing by the hour. The physics don't allow it.

But worse, linear trades often have **Uncapped Downsides**. If the economy tanks, or AI replaces your department, your income goes to zero instantly.

So, you are in a game with limited winnings and total ruin. That is a sucker's bet.

**The Holy Grail: Capped Downside, Infinite Upside**

To break out, you must shift your life into **Convex/Asymmetric Trades.**

An asymmetric trade is a scenario where the potential payoff is exponentially higher than the cost of playing.

**Examples of Asymmetry:**

1. **Writing a piece of Software:**
    - *The Cost (Downside):* 3 months of late nights and some caffeine.
    - *The Payoff (Upside):* Millions of users, acquisition by Google, or a recurring revenue stream that pays you while you sleep.
    - *The Math:* You risked time. You gained a fortune.
2. **Creating Media (This Book, a YouTube Channel, a Blog):**
    - *The Cost:* Effort and zero dollars.
    - *The Payoff:* Viral explosion, ad revenue, brand deals, global reach.
    - *The Math:* Capped risk, infinite scale.
3. **Angel Investing / Speculation:**
    - *The Cost:* Losing $1,000 (money you can afford to lose).
    - *The Payoff:* The startup becomes Uber. The coin goes 1000x.
    - *The Math:* You can only lose 1x your money, but you can make 1000x.

Do you see the difference? In the linear world, you work to *maintain.* In the asymmetric world, you work to *hit a jackpot.*

**The Barbell Strategy**

Now, I can hear your fear. "But I can't quit my job! I have rent!"

Good. Don't quit. Not yet.

You are going to use a strategy popularized by risk analyst Nassim Taleb called **The Barbell Strategy**.

Imagine a weightlifting barbell. It has weights on the two extremes, but nothing in the middle.

- **On one end (90%): Extreme Safety.** Keep your day job. Keep your cash in a boring savings account. Don't rack up credit card debt. Be hyper-conservative. This keeps you alive.
- **On the other end (10%): Extreme Risk.** Use your spare time, your weekends, and your discretionary income to place highly aggressive asymmetric bets.
- **The Middle (0%): Avoid Average Risk.** Avoid "moderate" risks like buying a fancy car on credit, or investing in stocks that yield 4% returns, or taking a slightly better job for slightly more money. The middle is where the slow lane kills you.

You want to be a boring accountant from 9-to-5, and a maniacal startup founder from 6-to-midnight.

The 90% protects you from ruin. The 10% exposes you to the **Black Swan.**

**Hunting the Black Swan**

A "Black Swan" is a rare, unpredictable event that carries an extreme impact.

In the financial world, most people are terrified of Black Swans (like a market crash). But we are **Hyper-Speed Wealth Seekers**. We are *hunting* for positive Black Swans.

We are looking for that one viral video, that one crypto spike, that one product launch that catches fire.

You cannot predict when a Black Swan will arrive. You cannot force a video to go viral. You cannot force a stock to moon.

**But you can stand in the rain with a bucket.**

Most people are standing inside, dry and safe, waiting for money to slide under the door. You need to be outside, placing as many asymmetric bets as possible (publishing content, launching products, making small investments).

You are buying lottery tickets where the odds are actually in your favor because *you own the lottery machine.*

**The "Overnight" Illusion**

This brings us back to the title of the book. How do you become a millionaire overnight?

You place asymmetric bets for 6 months, 12 months, or 2 years without seeing a result. You survive on your "Safe" income. You look like a failure.

Then, one of your bets hits.

The software takes off. The video hits the algorithm. The asset spikes.

Suddenly, you make $500,000 in a week.

The world looks at you and says, "Wow, an overnight success!"

They didn't see the asymmetry. They didn't see the Barbell. They only saw the Event.

**Actionable Takeaway: The Income Audit**

Put down the book. Pick up a pen.

Write down every source of income or potential income you have. Next to each, write "Linear" or "Asymmetric."

- *Consulting Client:* **Linear.** (If you stop, money stops. Capped upside).
- *Salary:* **Linear.** (Capped upside).
- *eBook on Amazon:* **Asymmetric.** (Write once, sell forever. Infinite upside).
- *Crypto Portfolio:* **Asymmetric.** (High risk, high reward).

**The Mission:** Your goal for the next 30 days is not to "make more money." It is to **alter the ratio.**

If 100% of your energy is going into Linear buckets, you will never be rich fast. You need to carve out time, brutally, if necessary, to start filling the Asymmetric bucket.

Stop trying to work harder. Start trying to bet smarter.

# Chapter 3: Killing the Hourly Wage

## Divorce Your Income from the Clock

Time is the only asset you have that is strictly finite. You can get more money. You can get more friends. You can get more property. You cannot get more time.

Yet, the vast majority of the population, including "successful" professionals, commit the ultimate financial sin: **They sell their time for money.**

They put a price tag on their life. $20 an hour. $50 an hour. $500 an hour.

It doesn't matter how high the number is. If your income is tied to your time, you are mathematically capped. There are only 24 hours in a day. Even if you bill $10,000 an hour, you have a ceiling. You are swimming with an anchor tied to your waist.

To achieve Hyper-Speed Wealth, you must kill the hourly wage. You must perform a surgical separation between *what you do* and *what you earn.*

## The Doctor is a Laborer

Let's shatter a common illusion.

Society tells you that a brain surgeon is "wealthy" and an Uber driver is "poor."

In the context of the Midnight Breakout, they are exactly the same.

They are both **Laborers**.

If the Uber driver stops driving, the app stops paying.

If the surgeon stops cutting, the hospital stops paying.

They are both hamsters on a wheel. The surgeon just has a better wheel made of mahogany and gold. But if either of them steps off to sleep, travel, or get sick, the income crashes to zero.

The **CEO Mindset**, the mindset you must adopt today, is different. The true CEO doesn't get paid for what they *do*. They get paid for the *system they built.*

You need to stop asking, "How can I work more hours?"

You need to start asking, "How can I disconnect my effort from my reward?"

## The Sleep Test

If you cannot make money while you are unconscious, you will work until you die.

This is the **Scalability** problem.

In a linear job (selling time), serving one customer takes X time. Serving 10 customers takes 10X time.

This is flawed by design. You cannot scale linearity.

To explode overnight, you need a vehicle that can serve 10,000 customers with the same effort it takes to serve one.

- **Flawed:** A personal trainer. (Can only train one person at a time).
- **Scalable:** A pre-recorded fitness program. (Can be downloaded by 1 million people simultaneously).
- **Flawed:** A cafe owner. (Limited by square footage and coffee beans).
- **Scalable:** Selling the *franchise rights* or a *branded coffee line.*

If your current path requires your physical presence to generate a dollar, you are not building a business. You are building a job. And jobs don't create dynasties.

## The Leverage Triad

How do you break the link between time and money? **Leverage.**

Archimedes said, "Give me a lever long enough, and I will move the world."

In business, leverage is what allows you to move millions of dollars with a gentle push.

There are three forms of leverage. The first two are old; the third is the key to the Midnight Breakout.

1. Labor Leverage (People)

This is the classic model. You hire people to work for you. You pay them \$20/hr., and you sell their work for \$50/hr. You pocket the spread.

- *Pros:* proven model.
- *Cons:* People are messy. They get sick, they sue you, they require management. Scaling people is slow and expensive.

2. Capital Leverage (Money)

This is the Wall Street model. You use money to make more money. You invest in factories, stocks, or real estate.

- *Pros:* Very passive once set up.
- *Cons:* You need money to play this game. If you are reading this book to *get* rich, you probably don't have enough capital yet to use this lever effectively.

3. The New Leverage: Code and Media

This is the atomic bomb of wealth creation. This is how the "Overnight Success" is manufactured.

- **Code:** Software, apps, algorithms, SAAS.

- **Media:** Books, blogs, YouTube videos, podcasts, digital courses.

**This leverage is Permissionless.** You don't need a bank to give you money (Capital). You don't need to interview employees (Labor). You just need a laptop.

**This leverage has Zero Marginal Cost of Replication.**

If you write a piece of code, it costs you nothing to let a million people use it.

If you record a video, it costs you nothing if ten million people watch it.

The Code/Media lever works for you 24/7/365. It never complains. It never asks for a raise. It creates value while you sleep.

The billionaires of the past (Carnegie, Rockefeller) used Labor and Capital.

The billionaires of today and tomorrow (you) will use Code and Media.

## The Great Detachment

Your goal is to become the Architect, not the Bricklayer.

The Bricklayer is paid by the hour. The Architect is paid for the design. Once the design is done, the Architect can sell that same blueprint a thousand times.

You must audit your life and look for the "levers." If you are doing a task that only produces value *once*, stop doing it. Or automate it. Or hire someone else to do it.

You must only work on things that produce value *repeatedly*.

- Building a sales funnel (Works repeatedly).
- Writing a sales email sequence (Works repeatedly).
- Creating a product (Works repeatedly).
- Answering a customer support call (Value dies when you hang

up).

## Actionable Takeaway: The Time Audit

I want you to track every single thing you do for the next 48 hours. Every email, every meeting, every task.

Then, create a spreadsheet with three columns:

1. **$10/hr. Tasks:** Answering generic emails, scheduling, data entry, cleaning, running errands.
2. **$100/hr. Tasks:** Project management, sales calls, skilled labor.
3. **$10,000/hr. Tasks:** Creating strategy, recording content, designing a product, setting up an automated funnel.

**The Rule:**

If you are doing $10/hr. tasks, you are essentially paying yourself minimum wage to be your own secretary. Stop it.

- **Delete** the task if it doesn't make money.
- **Delegate** the task to cheap labor or software if it must be done.
- **Focus** exclusively on the $10,000/hr. tasks.

You cannot earn a million dollars doing ten-dollar work. Kill the hourly wage before it kills your ambition.

# Chapter 4: The Sniper's Patience

## The Art of Active Waiting

In Hollywood war movies, the action hero is usually the guy running through the jungle with a machine gun, screaming at the top of his lungs, spraying bullets in every direction. He looks busy. He looks heroic. He creates a lot of noise.

In modern warfare, that guy is the first one to die.

The most dangerous person on the battlefield is the one you cannot see. He lies motionless in the mud for three days. He slows his heart rate. He calculates wind speed, earth rotation, and distance. He waits. And waits. And waits.

Then, he moves his finger one millimeter.

*Crack.*

Target down. Mission accomplished.

Most aspiring entrepreneurs are machine gunners. They are addicted to "Hustle Culture." They measure success by how much they sweat. They post on social media about their 16-hour days. They launch five half-baked businesses a year. They spray bullets everywhere and hit nothing.

To achieve the Midnight Breakout, you must trade the machine gun for the rifle. You must stop trying to force the market and start waiting for the market to expose its neck.

## The Bamboo Paradox

There is a species of Chinese Bamboo that frustrates every amateur gardener.

You plant the seed. You water it. You fertilize it. You stare at the ground.

For the first year, nothing happens. No sprout.

Second year. Nothing.

Third year. Nothing.

Fourth year. Nothing.

Most people quit here. They scream at the dirt. They assume the seed is dead. They assume the "system" is broken. They go back to planting potatoes because potatoes grow fast (but potatoes are cheap).

But in the fifth year, something terrifying happens. The bamboo shoot breaks the surface. And then, in a span of six weeks, it shoots up **90 feet into the air.**

Did the bamboo grow 90 feet in six weeks?

No. It grew 90 feet in five years.

If it had shot up in the first year without the massive root system it built during those four years of "nothing," the weight of the stalk would have snapped it in half.

The "Overnight Success" is the 90-foot growth spurt.

The "Sniper's Patience" is the root system.

You are currently in the root phase. You are building the infrastructure (the leverage, the skills, the audience) that will support the wealth when it arrives. If you get the money before you have the roots, the money will crush you. (We call this the Lottery Winner Curse, see Chapter 15).

**Active Waiting vs. Passive Laziness**

Do not mistake patience for laziness. They are opposites.

Laziness is watching Netflix and hoping a bag of cash falls through the ceiling.

**Active Waiting** is a state of high alert.

Think of a lioness in the tall grass. She is perfectly still, but she is not sleeping. Every muscle is coiled. Her eyes are tracking the herd. She is calculating which gazelle is the slowest, which way the wind is blowing, and exactly when the gap will open.

While you are waiting for your "Event", that viral spike, that crypto bull run, that acquisition offer, you are:

1. **Hoarding Cash:** So you have dry powder when the asset price crashes.
2. **Acquiring Skills:** So you can code the app in a weekend when

the idea hits.

3. **Building Networks:** So you have the phone numbers ready to dial when you need leverage.
4. **Testing:** Firing small tracer bullets (low risk) to see where the target is.

You are not doing *nothing*. You are accumulating **Potential Energy**.

The Breakout is when you convert that Potential Energy into **Kinetic Energy**.

**Trigger Discipline**

The hardest part of being a sniper isn't the waiting. It's the shooting.

When the moment arrives, when the "Event" window opens, you must act with violence and speed. You cannot hesitate.

There are two ways to fail at Trigger Discipline:

**1. The Premature Shot (FOMO)**

You get bored. You haven't seen results in three months. You see your friends making money on a trend that is already dying. You panic. You go "All In" on a bad bet just to feel like you're in the game. You miss. You lose your capital. Now, when the *real* opportunity comes, you have no bullets left.

**2. The Hesitation (Fear)**

The opportunity is right in front of you. The housing market crashes 40%. The crypto coin dumps 80%. This is what you waited for. But now, fear sets in. "What if it goes lower?" "What if I'm wrong?"

You freeze.

The window closes. The price recovers. The opportunity is gone forever.

The Sniper waits months for a window that stays open for three seconds. In those three seconds, he does not think. He executes.

**The Illusion of "Suddenly"**

When you finally pull the trigger and your bank account swells from four figures to seven figures in a few weeks, the world will hate you.

They will say, "He got lucky."

They will say, "It happened so fast."

They will say, "It's not fair."

Let them talk. They didn't see you lying in the mud. They didn't see the roots growing underground. They didn't see the years of Active Waiting where you denied yourself instant gratification to position yourself for this single moment.

Wealth is a transfer mechanism from the impatient to the patient.

The market is volatile. It moves in waves. The "Steady" worker tries to paddle against the waves every day. The Surfer (The Sniper) sits on his board, bobbing up and down, ignoring the small ripples, waiting for the rogue wave.

When the big one comes, he doesn't paddle steadily. He paddles explosively. He catches it. And he rides it all the way to the shore.

**Actionable Takeaway: The Trigger Event**

You cannot hit a target you haven't defined. You need to write down your **Rules of Engagement**.

Stop saying, "I want to invest in Real Estate."

Stop saying, "I want to start a business."

Those are vague wishes. Snipers deal in coordinates.

Write down your **Trigger Event**:

- *Example (Investor):* "I am holding $50,000 in cash. I will buy Bitcoin ONLY if it drops below $X. If it does not, I do nothing."
- *Example (Entrepreneur):* "I will launch my product ONLY when I have 1,000 people on the waitlist. Until then, I do not write a line of code; I only market."
- *Example (Trader):* "I will exit this position and take profit when the price hits $Y. I will not get greedy."

Define the condition. Wait for the condition.

When the condition is met, fire.

# Chapter 5: The Digital Multiplier

## Escaping the Tyranny of Atoms

There are two worlds you can do business in.

**World A is the World of Atoms.**

In this world, things are heavy. They take up space. They rot. They break during shipping. If you sell chairs, and you want to sell 1,000 chairs, you have to build 1,000 chairs. You need wood, screws, glue, a factory, a warehouse, and a shipping container.

If you sell 10,000 chairs, you might go bankrupt trying to fulfill the orders because you run out of cash buying the wood.

The World of Atoms has **Friction.** Friction is the enemy of Speed.

**World B is the World of Bits.**

In this world, things are weightless. They take up zero space. They travel at the speed of light. If you sell a piece of software, and you want to sell 1,000 copies, you press "Enter."

If you sell 10,000 copies? You press "Enter."

If you sell 10 million copies? You press "Enter."

The cost to replicate the product is zero. The time to deliver the product is zero.

The World of Bits has **No Friction.**

If you want to get rich slowly, sell atoms. Open a bakery. Start a clothing line. Enjoy your 12% profit margins and your back pain.

If you want to get rich overnight, you must live in the World of Bits. You must harness the **Digital Multiplier**.

## Zero Marginal Cost of Replication

This is the most important economic concept for the modern wealth seeker.

**Marginal Cost** is the cost to produce *one extra unit* of whatever you are selling.

- For Ford to make one extra F-150 truck, it costs them $30,000 in parts and labor.
- For a restaurant to serve one extra steak, it costs them $15 in meat and chef time.

But for a creator of digital products, the marginal cost is **zero**.

Let's say you write a piece of code (SaaS) or record an online course.

The "First Unit" is expensive. It might take you 500 hours and $5,000 to create that first version. You are bleeding time and money.

But the "Second Unit"? **Free.**

The "Millionth Unit"? **Free.**

Once the asset exists, it is detached from labor. You have built a money printing press where the ink costs nothing.

This creates a phenomenon called **Infinite Leverage**. In the physical world, revenue is tied to COGS (Cost of Goods Sold). In the digital world, revenue is decoupled from cost. As you scale, your profit margin doesn't just stay the same; it expands towards 100%.

## The Infinite Shelf

In the old world, if you wanted to sell a book, you had to convince a Barnes & Noble manager to put it on a shelf.

That shelf is expensive real estate. If your book didn't sell fast enough, they took it down to make room for Stephen King.

This meant you could only sell "Mass Market" products. You had to please everyone to earn the shelf space. And when you try to please everyone, you please no one.

The Internet is an **Infinite Shelf**.

It costs Amazon nothing to list your eBook. It costs Apple nothing to host your app.

This means you don't need to compete with Coca-Cola or Stephen King. You can go narrow. You can go niche.

You can write a software plugin that only solves a problem for "Dentists in Canada who use MacBook."

In the physical world, that market is too small to justify a store.

In the digital world, that market is a gold mine. You can reach every single one of them instantly, with zero rent and zero overhead.

## The Trinity of Digital Assets

So, what are we selling? We aren't drop shipping cheap plastic toothbrushes from China (that's atoms, that's friction). We are building assets.

**1. Software (SaaS - Software as a Service)**

This is the apex predator of wealth. You build a tool that solves a recurring problem. People pay you a monthly subscription to use it.

- *Why it wins:* Recurring revenue. You sell the customer once, and they pay you every month for years. It is the closest thing to legal crack cocaine.

**2. Information (Courses/eBooks)**

You package your knowledge into a format that can be downloaded.

- *Why it wins:* 100% Margin. It is literally selling air. If you sell a PDF for $50, you keep $49.50 (after credit card fees). There is no shipping, no returns, no broken parts.

**3. Templates & Tools**

Selling "Speed." People are lazy. They don't want to build a spreadsheet, a legal contract, or a design file from scratch.

- *Why it wins:* High utility. You aren't selling "education"; you are selling a "done-for-you" result.

## Pricing Power: The 99% Margin

When you sell atoms, your price is dictated by your costs. If the chair costs $50 to make, you have to sell it for $100.

When you sell bits, your price is dictated by **Value**.

If your $0-cost digital course helps a business owner save $10,000 on their taxes, can you charge $1,000 for it?

Yes.

Does it matter that it only cost you $0 to send them the file?

No.

The customer is paying for the *result*, not the *materials*.

Because your margins are 90-99%, you have a strategic advantage in advertising. You can afford to spend more to acquire a customer than your physical competitors.

If you sell a $100 digital product, you can afford to spend $90 on ads to get that customer and still make a profit.

If a physical store sells a $100 shoe, they can only spend $10 on ads.

**You win the war because your weapon is lighter.**

## Actionable Takeaway: The Digital Blueprint

You are not going to build the "Next Facebook." That is a lottery ticket.

You are going to build a "Micro-Asset" that solves a painful, expensive problem for a specific group of people.

**The Exercise:**

1. **Identify a Niche:** Do not pick "Fitness." Pick "Post-pregnancy weight loss for working moms."
2. **Identify the Pain:** What is the thing they hate doing? (e.g., "I don't have time to cook healthy meals").
3. **Create the Digital Solution:**
    - *The eBook:* "15-Minute Meals for Moms."
    - *The Template:* A printable grocery list and meal planner.

    - *The App:* A simple timer/reminder tool for water intake.

**Your Homework:**

Draft a one-page blueprint for a digital product you could create this weekend.

- **Format:** (PDF, Video, Spreadsheet, Code)
- **Price:** (How much is the problem worth to solve?)
- **Audience:** (Who is holding the credit card?)

Stop thinking about how to *work* for money. Start thinking about what you can *create* that will work for you.

# Chapter 6: The Virality Jackpot

**Compressing Decades into Days**

In the old world, the world of your parents, building a brand took thirty years. You bought a billboard. You took out an ad in the Yellow Pages. You shook hands at the Rotary Club. You grew your reputation one agonizingly slow conversation at a time.

Today, that model is a horse and buggy on a Formula 1 track.

We live in the era of the **Algorithm**. The Algorithm is a blind, impartial deity. It does not care who your father is. It does not care if you have a degree. It cares about one thing: **Retention.**

If you can keep a stranger staring at a screen for 15 seconds, the Algorithm will reward you by showing your face to 10,000 more people. If they stare, it shows you to 100,000. Then 10 million.

In 48 hours, you can reach more people than a stadium rock band reaches in a twenty-year career.

This is the **Virality Jackpot**. It is the single most potent mechanism for hyper-speed wealth because it solves the hardest problem in business: Distribution.

**Attention is the New Oil**

Stop thinking about money. Start thinking about eyeballs.

In the current economy, **Attention is the primary asset.** Money is secondary. Money *follows* attention.

If you have the attention of a million people, you can sell them t-shirts, software, consulting, or supplements. You can sell them *anything*. If you have the best product in the world but zero attention, you are broke.

The "Slow Lane" approach to marketing is paying for attention (Ads). You pay Facebook $1 to get a customer. You hope they spend $2. It's reliable, but it's expensive and slow.

The "Fast Lane" approach is **Organic Virality**. It is free, and it scales vertically.

When a piece of content goes viral, you are effectively siphoning millions of dollars of free advertising from the platform. You are hacking the system to work for you.

**Content Arbitrage: Don't Be Original, Be Adaptive**

How do you go viral? Do you need to be a genius auteur?

No. You need to be a **Trader**.

Traders look for patterns. In the content game, we call this **Content Arbitrage.**

You don't need to invent a new format. You need to look at what the market is currently rewarding.

- Is the market rewarding 7-second looping videos with text overlays?
- Is it rewarding long-form Twitter threads breaking down historical events?
- Is it rewarding POV videos of pressure washing driveways?

Find the wave that is already cresting and put your surfboard on it.

This isn't plagiarism; it's adaptation. If a specific audio track is trending on TikTok, use it *immediately* to showcase your product. If a specific meme format is blowing up on LinkedIn, rewrite it for your industry.

The "Artist" waits for inspiration. The "Viral Engineer" looks at the data, sees what the Algorithm craves today, and feeds the beast.

**The Funnel: Turning Views into Vaults**

Here is where 99% of "Influencers" fail. They get the views, but they stay broke.

They get the **Virality Jackpot** (10 million views), but they have no bucket to catch the rain. They get a dopamine hit, but their bank account doesn't move.

To become a millionaire overnight, you need a mechanism that instantly converts **Attention into Cash.**

This is the **High-Speed Funnel**:

1. **The Bait (The Viral Video):** A hook that grabs 10 million people.
2. **The Call to Action (CTA):** The last 3 seconds of the video must scream, "Link in Bio for the Solution."
3. **The Capture (The Landing Page):** A simple, frictionless page that takes their email or their credit card.
4. **The Product (The Digital Multiplier):** The eBook, Course, or SaaS you built in Chapter 5.

Imagine this scenario:

You post a video about "How to fix back pain in 30 seconds."

It goes viral. 5 million views.

1% of viewers click your profile. (50,000 people).

10% of those click the link to your "$29 Back Pain Relief Guide." (5,000 people).

10% of those buy. (500 people).

500 sales x 29 = 14,500 in one day.

From one video. That took you 20 minutes to film on your phone.

Now imagine you do that twice a week. That is the math of hyper-speed wealth.

**Actionable Takeaway: The "Sticky" Framework**

You are going to create your first piece of "Weaponized Content" today. Use this 3-step framework designed for conversion, not just entertainment.

**1. The Hook (0:00 - 0:03)**

You must stop the scroll. Do not say "Hi guys, welcome to my channel." That is death.

- *Visual:* Sudden movement, weird angle, or text that flashes a controversial statement.
- *Verbal:* "Stop doing [Common Habit] immediately." or "Here is why you will never be rich."
- *Goal:* Create an "Open Loop" in their brain that they *must*

close by watching.

**2. The Value (0:03 - 0:45)**
Deliver on the promise of the hook. Fast cuts. No "umms" or "ahhs."

- Give them the tip, the secret, or the story.
- Keep the pacing rapid. If you bore them for a second, they swipe away.

**3. The Ask (0:45 - End)**
You are not here to be their friend. You are here to do business.

- "If you want the full step-by-step list, I put it in the document in my bio."
- "I built a tool that does this for you. Link in profile."

**The Assignment:**
Spend 30 minutes scrolling TikTok or Reels. Find a video in your niche with over 100k likes.

Reverse engineer it. Why did it work?

Re-record that exact concept with your own face, your own voice, and your own product pitch.

Post it.

Repeat until the Jackpot hits.

# Chapter 7: The Speculator's Edge

**Surfing the Chaos**

Let's address the elephant in the room. You have been told that buying cryptocurrency, trading options, or betting on volatile penny stocks is "gambling."

Your parents say it. Your financial advisor says it. The broke guy at the bar says it.

They are half-right. When *they* do it, it is gambling. When *you* do it, armed with the principles of this chapter, it is **Speculation**.

The difference between a Gambler and a Speculator is simple:

The Gambler seeks *excitement* and relies on *hope*.

The Speculator seeks *inefficiency* and relies on *math*.

To become a millionaire overnight, you cannot park your money in a diverse portfolio of blue-chip stocks and wait for 8% annual returns. You need **Volatility**. You need chaos. You need markets that move 50%, 100%, or 1000% in a week.

Volatility is not risk; volatility is the engine of speed.

**The prediction Trap**

The biggest mistake amateurs make in high-speed markets (Crypto/Options) is trying to be Nostradamus.

"I *think* Bitcoin is going to $100,000."

"I *feel* like Tesla is due for a bounce."

Your thoughts and feelings are irrelevant. The market does not care about your intuition.

The Speculator does not predict. The Speculator **reacts**.

This is called **Trend Following**.

If the market is ripping upward, you buy. You ride the wave.

If the market turns downward, you sell. You get off the wave.

You do not argue with the ocean. You do not try to command the tide. You simply look at the chart. Is the line going up? Get in. Is the line breaking down? Get out.

The "Smart Money" spends millions on algorithms to predict the future. You don't have millions. But you have agility. You can enter and exit a trade in seconds. That is your edge.

**Information Asymmetry: The Speed of Truth**

In the stock market of the 1990s, everyone got the news at the same time (the morning paper). The market was somewhat "efficient."

In the Wild West of Crypto and small-cap assets, the market is wildly inefficient.

There is a hierarchy of information speed:

1. **The Insiders:** The developers, the VCs, the inner circle. (They know instantly).
2. **The On-Chain Sleuths:** The people tracking wallet movements on the blockchain. (They know minutes later).
3. **The Twitter/Discord Elite:** The hyper-active niche communities. (They know hours later).
4. **Mainstream Media (CNBC/Forbes):** They report it 3 days later.

**Rule of Thumb:** If you are reading about a "hot new token" on a major news website, it is too late. You are not the investor; you are the **Exit Liquidity**. The early adopters are selling *to* you.

To catch the spike, you must move upstream. You must inhabit the places where news breaks *before* it becomes news. You must be in the Discords, watching the wallets, and reading the raw data.

**The Shield: Mathematics of Ruin**

The only thing that matters in speculation is **Staying in the Game**.

If you lose 100% of your money, you are dead. You cannot bet again. Game over.

Therefore, your primary job is not making money; it is **protecting your capital**.

You must use **Stop Losses**.

A Stop Loss is a mechanical tripwire. "If I buy this asset at $100, and it drops to $90, I sell immediately. No questions asked."

The Amateur holds a losing bag, praying it will go back up. "It's just a dip!" he screams as it goes to zero.

The Speculator takes the small loss (10%), keeps 90% of his capital, and looks for the next trade.

**The Golden Ratio:**

Never risk more than 1% to 5% of your total net worth on a single speculative trade.

If you have $10,000, do not put $10,000 into a crypto coin. Put $500.

If that $500 goes to $0, you are still alive.

If that $500 goes to $50,000 (a 100x return), you have changed your life.

This is the Barbell Strategy from Chapter 2 applied to trading. Capped downside (you lose $500). Infinite upside (you make $50k).

**Actionable Takeaway: The Speculation Fund**

You are forbidden from touching your rent money. You are forbidden from touching your grocery money.

**Step 1: Create the "Vegas Fund."**

Scrape together an amount of money you are mentally comfortable setting on fire. $500? $1,000? $5,000?

Transfer this to a separate brokerage or crypto wallet. This is your war chest.

**Step 2: Write the Constitution.**

On a piece of paper, write your immutable laws:

1. **The Stop:** "I will never stay in a trade that is down more than 15%."
2. **The Take:** "I will sell 50% of my position when it doubles to lock in my principal."
3. **The Source:** "I will not buy based on a YouTuber's advice. I will only buy based on price action."

**Step 3: The First Trade.**

Find a market with high volatility. Look for a trend that has *already started* (moving up). Enter small. Set your stop loss.

If you win, you don't buy a watch. You add it to the war chest.

If you lose, you analyze why, and you try again.

Welcome to the arena. Keep your shield up.

# Chapter 8: The "Flipping" Economy

### The Art of the Middleman

There is a pervasive myth that to get rich, you must be an "Inventor." You must be Elon Musk designing a rocket or Steve Jobs holding a prototype iPhone.

This is false. Inventors usually die broke, waiting for patents.

The fastest way to generate cash, immediate, liquid cash, is not to *create* value, but to *move* value.

This is the game of **Arbitrage**.

Arbitrage is the exploitation of a price difference between two markets. It is finding something that is undervalued in Place A and selling it for its true value in Place B.

You are not the manufacturer. You are not the end-user. You are the Bridge. And the Bridge gets paid a toll.

If you have zero capital and zero product, this is your starting line. You don't need an idea. You just need eyes to see the gap.

### The Inefficiency Hunter

Markets are not efficient. That is a lie told by economists who have never sold anything.

- A vintage chair on Facebook Marketplace is listed for $20 because the owner just wants it out of their garage. On eBay, collectors are buying that same chair for $400.
- A local dentist needs a website. He is willing to pay $2,000 because he is rich and busy. On Upwork, a developer in Eastern Europe is willing to build that website for $200.

The gap between $20 and $400, or $200 and $2,000, is called the **Spread**.

Most people see the chair and think, "That's cheap."

Most people see the dentist and think, "I can't build websites."

The Flipping Economy is about seeing the Spread. It is about understanding that value is subjective. The garage owner values *space*. The collector values the *chair*. You provide the space to one and the chair to the other, and you keep the difference.

**Service Arbitrage (Drop Servicing)**

Physical flipping (buying low, selling high) is great, but it requires shipping, storage, and logistics. It has friction.

**Service Arbitrage** has no friction.

You become a General Contractor for digital services.

You set up an agency selling "High-End Video Editing" for $1,000 a month.

Do you edit videos? Absolutely not.

You find a talented editor overseas who charges $300 a month.

You sell the service to the client. You pay the worker. You pocket the $700 spread.

You are selling **Trust** and **Convenience**. The client pays the premium because they don't want to scour freelance boards; they want *you* to handle it.

This scales infinitely. You can have 50 clients and 50 freelancers. You are just the hub of the wheel.

**Wholesaling: The Paper Game**

Now let's look at the heavy artillery: **Wholesaling.**

This is how people enter real estate with $0 in their bank account.

The concept is simple: You are not selling the house. You are selling the **Contract.**

1. **Find the Distress:** You find a homeowner who needs to sell *fast* (divorce, foreclosure, inherited house). The house is worth $200,000, but they will take $150,000 just to be done with it.
2. **Lock it Up:** You sign a contract with them to buy it for $150,000. The contract gives you 30 days to close.
3. **Find the Buyer:** You call a cash investor (a landlord or house flipper). You say, "I have a house under contract for $150k. It's

yours for $160k."

4. **The Assign:** You assign the contract to the investor.
5. **The Payday:** At closing, the seller gets their $150k. The investor gets the house. The title company cuts *you* a check for $10,000.

You never owned the house. You never took out a mortgage. You never fixed a toilet.

You flipped the paper.

This applies to businesses too. You can find a business for sale, put it under contract, and flip the contract to a larger competitor.

**Speed of Implementation**

The "Flipping Economy" has one enemy: **Time.**

Inefficiencies do not last forever.

If a chair is underpriced, someone else will buy it.

If a niche is underserved, someone else will fill it.

The winner in arbitrage is not the smartest; it is the **Fastest**.

You cannot analyze a flip for two weeks. By the time you decide, the deal is gone. You must develop the instinct to pull the trigger.

This is high-velocity capital turnover.

In the stock market, you wait a year for 10%.

In a flip, you wait 24 hours for 100%.

If you start with $1,000 and flip it for 20% profit once a week, compounding that weekly, you will have an astronomical sum by the end of the year. That is the power of high-frequency turnover.

**Actionable Takeaway: The Weekend Arbitrage**

You are going to execute a flip this weekend.

**Option A: The Physical Flip**

1. Open Facebook Marketplace or Craigslist.
2. Search for "Free" or deeply discounted items (Furniture, Electronics, Gym Equipment).
3. Look up the sold prices of those same items on eBay.

4. If the Spread is >$100, go get it. Clean it. List it.

**Option B: The Service Flip**

1. Go to a local business networking group or browse LinkedIn. Find a business that has terrible copy, no logo, or a broken website.
2. Offer to fix it for a set price (e.g., $500).
3. Once they pay (or agree), go to Fiverr or Upwork and pay someone $50 to do the work.
4. Deliver the work. Keep the $450.

Do not overthink it. Find the gap. Build the bridge. Collect the toll.

# Chapter 9: The Acquisition

**The Exit is the Product**

There is a romantic notion in business that you should build a company to pass down to your grandchildren. A "Legacy." A monument to your ego.

Forget that.

Grandchildren are ungrateful, and legacies are heavy. If you want hyper-speed wealth, you are not building a company to keep. You are building a company to **sell**.

The "Midnight Breakout" often happens in a lawyer's conference room (or these days, via a DocuSign email) when a wire transfer hits your account for a sum larger than your parents earned in their combined lifetimes.

This is the **Acquisition**.

Most entrepreneurs treat the exit as an afterthought. "If someone wants to buy me, I guess I'll sell."

This is wrong. The Exit is not the *end* of the process; it is the *design* of the process.

You are not building a business to operate it. You are raising a pig to take it to market. If you get emotionally attached to the pig, you lose.

**The "Feature" Strategy**

How do you ensure someone buys you? You solve a problem that a giant company is too slow to solve themselves.

Big corporations (Google, Ford, Proctor & Gamble) are Titanics. They cannot turn. They cannot innovate fast.

You are a Speedboat.

Don't try to build a "better Google." You will die.

Instead, build a specific **feature** that Google is missing.

- **Don't** build a social network.
- **Do** build an AI tool that automatically moderates comments on social networks.

When you build a "Feature Business," you are effectively acting as the outsourced R&D department for a giant. You take the risk. You find the product-market fit.

Once it works, the Giant looks at you and does the math:

*"It will take us 2 years and $5 million to build this internally. Or we can buy this kid for $2 million tomorrow."*

They will buy you. Not because they love you, but because it is cheaper and faster than doing it themselves. You are selling them **speed.**

**The Magic of the Multiple**

Why is selling better than keeping?

**The Multiple.**

In the world of high finance, businesses are valued based on a multiple of their profit (EBITDA) or revenue.

Let's say you build a niche newsletter or a Shopify app that makes $100,000 a year in profit.

That is a nice income. It buys a nice car.

But you are still on the treadmill. You have to keep running to keep getting that $100k.

But if you **sell** that asset, the market might value it at a **5x Multiple.**

**100,000 x 5= 500,000.**

In one signature, you collect **five years of future work.**

You have time-traveled. You have pulled five years of income into the present moment, tax-efficiently (capital gains tax is usually lower than income tax).

If you are in a hot sector (like AI or SaaS), that multiple can go to **10x or 20x Revenue.**

Suddenly, your $100k/year side hustle is a $2 Million exit.

That is how you become a millionaire overnight. You don't save the cash flow. You sell the asset.

**The Rise of the Aggregators**

"But who will buy my small business?"

In the past, you needed a strategic buyer like Microsoft.

Today, we have **Aggregators.**

These are investment firms (Micro-Private Equity) raised specifically to buy small, profitable internet businesses.

- **Thrasio** buys Amazon FBA brands.
- **Tiny Capital** buys simple internet agencies and software.
- **Flippa** and **Micro Acquire** are marketplaces where you can list your startup like a used car.

There is a hunger for yield. Investors are sitting on trillions of dollars of "dry powder." They can't get good returns in the bond market. They are desperate to buy cash-flowing digital assets.

They don't care about your brand's "soul." They care about your spreadsheets. If the math works, they wire the money.

**The "Unsellable" Trap**

Warning: Most small businesses are worthless.

Why? **Because the owner is the business.**

If you are a consultant and you sell "John Smith Consulting," nobody can buy that. If John Smith leaves, the revenue leaves.

You have built a job, not an asset.

To make your business sellable, you must make yourself irrelevant.

- **Document everything:** Standard Operating Procedures (SOPs).
- **Automate everything:** The software should run without you.
- **Brand it abstractly:** Don't call it "John's Cookies." Call it "Midnight Cookies."

The buyer is buying the *machine*, not the *operator*. If the machine requires you to turn the crank, it has a multiple of zero.

**Actionable Takeaway: The Pre-Mortem Exit List**

Before you write a single line of code or buy a single unit of inventory, you must know who is going to buy you out.

**The Exercise:**

Write down the names of **5 Specific Companies** that would benefit from owning what you are about to build.

- *If you are building a fitness app:*
    1. Nike (needs digital community)
    2. MyFitnessPal (needs new features)
    3. Peloton (needs add-ons)
    4. Private Equity Firm X (aggregates health apps)
    5. Insurance Company Y (wants user health data)

If you cannot list 5 buyers, **do not build the business.** You are building a dead-end street.

Build the road that leads directly to their front door.

# Chapter 10: Building the Trap

**Infrastructure for the Flood**

There is a specific type of tragedy that is funnier than failure, but more painful.

It is the **Success Disaster.**

Imagine this: You finally hit the jackpot. The influencer shouts you out. The algorithm picks up your video. The crypto token pumps. You have 50,000 people flooding your website in the span of ten minutes, waving their credit cards, begging to give you money.

And then... the screen goes white.

*Error 503: Service Unavailable.*

Your cheap $5/month hosting plan just melted.

Your payment processor freezes your funds because they suspect "fraud" due to the velocity of sales.

Your email server crashes.

By the time you wake up and fix it, the mob is gone. The viral moment has passed. You didn't catch lightning in a bottle; you caught it in a paper cup, and it burned your house down.

You must stop building for "slow growth." You must stop building for the 10 visitors a day you have now.

You are here to engineer a Midnight Breakout. You must build a **Trap** capable of holding the beast when it finally steps in.

**Load Bearing: The Concrete Foundation**

Most "solopreneurs" build their infrastructure with duct tape and hope. They use the cheapest hosting, the free version of plugins, and fragile code.

This is acceptable for a hobby. It is suicide for a Breakout.

When the flood comes, it comes all at once. This is the **DDOS of Success.**

You need to ask yourself a terrifying question: **What happens if I get 10,000 orders in one hour?**

1. **The Server:** If you are on shared hosting (Bluehost, GoDaddy basic plans), you are dead. You need scalable cloud hosting (AWS, dedicated Shopify servers, or premium managed hosting like Kinsta/WP Engine) that auto-scales bandwidth.
2. **The Payment Gateway:** This is the silent killer. Stripe and PayPal have automated fraud detection algorithms. If a brand new account suddenly processes $50,000 in an hour, their robots will lock your account.
    - *The Fix:* **Warm up the account.** Or, contact their support *before* the launch to warn them of the expected volume. Have a backup payment processor (a "Merchant Account") ready to switch on if the primary one freezes.

You are building a skyscraper. Do not pour a foundation made of sand.

**Frictionless Conversion: Greasing the Slide**

Every extra click between the "I want this" thought and the "Transaction Complete" screen costs you money.

We call this **Friction.**

During a viral spike, attention spans are microscopic. People are clicking from TikTok or Instagram. They are on their phones. They are distracted.

If your website asks them to "Create an Account" before buying... **you lose 40% of them.**

If your page takes 4 seconds to load... **you lose 30% of them.**

If they have to find their wallet to type in a 16-digit card number... **you lose 20% of them.**

Your job is to grease the slide.

- **Apple Pay / Google Pay:** This is mandatory. It allows people to pay with a fingerprint. No typing. No wallet. One second.
- **Guest Checkout:** Never force a login. Take the money first; let them set a password later.

- **One-Page Funnels:** The sales pitch, the form, and the checkout should ideally be on the same page. Don't make them click "Next."

A Breakout business does not have an "Add to Cart" button. It has a "Buy Now" button.

**Customer Support AI: The Robot Army**

If you sell 1,000 units in a night, you will get 100 emails the next morning asking, "Did it go through?" or "Where is my download?"

If you try to answer these yourself, you will spend the next three weeks in email hell. You will miss the opportunity to capitalize on the momentum because you are too busy playing janitor.

You cannot scale humans instantly. But you can scale **AI Agents**.

Before you launch, you must install the infrastructure of automation.

- **The Chatbot:** Set up Intercom, Drift, or an AI agent trained on your FAQs. It should answer 90% of queries (refunds, shipping times, download links) without a human ever seeing them.
- **The Auto-Responder Sequence:** Your email provider should instantly send a receipt, a welcome guide, and a "What to expect next" email.

People today do not demand human empathy. They demand **speed**. If a bot solves their problem in 2 seconds, they are happier than if a human solves it in 2 hours.

Build the robot army before the war starts.

**Actionable Takeaway: The "Stress Test" Checklist**

Do not launch until you have checked every box on this list.

**1. The Speed Test**

- Go to *Google Page Speed Insights*. Is your mobile score above 90?

- If not, compress your images. Remove heavy scripts.

**2. The Mobile Audit**

- Buy your own product on your phone.
- Do you have to pinch to zoom?
- Is the "Buy" button stuck under a pop-up?
- If it takes more than 60 seconds to buy, fail.

**3. The Gateway Defense**

- Do you have Apple Pay/Google Pay enabled?
- Do you have a backup payment option (e.g., PayPal) if Stripe fails?

**4. The Crash Test**

- Use a tool like *Loader.io* to simulate 1,000 visitors hitting your site at once.
- Does it crash? Upgrade your server plan today.

**5. The Zero-Human Test**

- Can a customer buy, receive the product, and get a receipt without you clicking a single button?
- If you have to manually "approve" anything, you are the bottleneck. Remove yourself.

The Trap is set. The bait is ready. Now, we wait for the beast.

# Chapter 11: The Launch Button

**Engineering the Frenzy**

Imagine two stores.

Store A has a bright neon sign that says "OPEN." The doors are wide. The shelves are stocked. You can walk in anytime, buy a shirt, and leave. You feel nothing. You might buy today, or you might buy next month. Who cares?

Store B has its windows blacked out. The door is locked. There is a line of 300 people shivering in the rain outside. A bouncer stands at the door holding a clipboard. A sign reads: *"Opening at Midnight. Limited Quantities. One per customer."*

Which store makes a million dollars in an hour?

Which store creates a riot?

Most entrepreneurs build Store A because they are desperate. They think, "I need to be available so people can pay me."

**Wrong.** Availability is the killer of desire.

To achieve a Midnight Breakout, you must understand a dark truth about human psychology: **We do not value what is abundant. We value what is scarce.**

You are not just releasing a product. You are orchestrating a **Drop**.

**The Cult of the Drop**

Look at Supreme. Look at the NFT markets of 2021. Look at high-end sneakers.

They created billions of dollars in wealth not by satisfying demand, but by **starving** it.

They mastered **Artificial Scarcity**.

In the digital world (Chapter 5), we established that your product has zero marginal cost. You can sell infinite copies.

But to trigger the "Launch Button," you must *pretend* your capacity is finite.

If you are selling a digital course, you don't say, "Enroll anytime!"

You say, "Class size is limited to 100 students due to bandwidth."

Or, "The cart closes in 48 hours and will not reopen until next year."

Is this true? Technologically, no.

Is it necessary? Psychologically, yes.

You must force the customer to make a binary decision: **Buy Now or Miss Out Forever.**

Without the threat of loss, there is no urgency. Without urgency, there is no velocity.

**The Velvet Rope**

The most powerful word in marketing is not "Free." It is **"Waitlist."**

Before you ever ask for a dollar, you must build a Velvet Rope. This changes the power dynamic.

- "Buy my product" = You are a beggar.
- "Join the waitlist for early access" = You are the prize.

You want people banging on the door before you unlock it. You want them refreshing their email inboxes at 11:59 PM.

This period of "Pre-Launch" is where you build the pressure. You show them the result (the lifestyle, the solution) but you deny them the mechanism. You let the pressure build in the pipes.

When you finally turn the valve (The Launch), the pressure releases in an explosion of sales. This is how you do $100,000 in a day instead of a year.

**FOMO Engineering**

Fear Of Missing Out (FOMO) is not a buzzword; it is a biological survival mechanism. In the wild, if the herd moved and you didn't, you got eaten.

You must weaponize this herd instinct.

**1. The Ticking Clock:**

There must be a deadline. A discount that expires. A bonus stack that disappears. A countdown timer on your page is not a decoration; it is a gun to the head of procrastination.

**2. Visual Velocity:**

"50% of spots claimed in the first hour!"
"Only 3 tickets left."
Show the inventory depleting in real-time.

**3. The Social Swarm:**

When the launch happens, you need noise. You need screenshots of people buying. You need Retweets. You need the "Validation Loop."

When a customer sees that *others* are buying, their logical brain shuts off and their lizard brain takes over. "Everyone is running this way; I must run too."

**Actionable Takeaway: The 7-Day Pressure Cooker**

Do not just "put your product online." That is a whisper. You need a scream.

Here is the exact email sequence to send to your waitlist (from Chapter 12) to engineer a Midnight Breakout.

**Day 1: The Tease (The "What")**

- Subject: *Something is coming...*
- Body: Don't sell. Just hint. "I've been working on something for 6 months that solves [Big Problem]. I'm almost ready to show you."

**Day 2: The Logic (The "Why")**

- Subject: *Why most people fail at [Topic]*
- Body: Agitate the pain. Explain why the current solutions suck. "The old way doesn't work. We need a new mechanism."

**Day 3: The Proof (The "Who")**

- Subject: *How Jane made $10k in a week*
- Body: Show a beta tester or a case study. "I let Jane try the new system. Here is what happened." (Builds credibility).

**Day 4: The Reveal (The "How")**

- Subject: *Introducing: The Breakout Protocol*
- Body: Reveal the product name and what it does. But they still can't buy. "I'm opening the doors on Tuesday at 9 AM EST."

**Day 5: The Scarcity (The "Catch")**

- Subject: *Bad news...*
- Body: "We only have 500 spots / The 50% discount is only for the first 24 hours." (Sets the hook).

**Day 6: The Warning (The "When")**

- Subject: *Tomorrow. 9:00 AM.*
- Body: "Get your credit card ready. This will sell out."

**Day 7: THE LAUNCH (The "Drop")**

- Subject: *WE ARE LIVE (Open)*
- Body: "The doors are open. The link is here. Go."

Then, you step back. And you watch the server load spike.

# Chapter 12: Network Leverage

**The Art of Borrowed Fire**

If you follow the advice of traditional marketing, you are doomed to the Slow Lane.

They tell you: "Post consistently. Engage with your community. Build trust brick by brick."

This works, if you have ten years. You don't. You want to break out by midnight.

Building an audience from scratch is the hardest, slowest, most expensive thing you can do in business. It is pushing a boulder uphill.

The smart money doesn't build the road; they hitch a ride on a truck that is already moving.

This is the principle of **OPA: Other People's Audiences.**

Right now, at this exact second, someone else has already gathered your customers. They have already earned their trust. They have already done the hard work of curating 100,000 people who love exactly what you are selling.

You don't need to build a stadium. You just need to get the microphone from the guy standing on stage.

**The Affiliate Army: Greed is Your Friend**

How do you get the microphone? You pay for it.

Many entrepreneurs are greedy. They want to keep 100% of the profit. They think, "I built the product, I deserve the money."

This is poor-person math.

**100% of Zero is Zero.**

I would rather have **50% of $1 Million** than **100% of $10,000.**

To create a viral explosion, you must build an **Affiliate Army**. You recruit other creators, newsletter writers, and influencers, and you offer them a deal that is shocking:

*"Sell my product, and keep 50% of the revenue."*

If you are selling a digital product (Chapter 5), your cost is zero. So giving away 50% doesn't hurt you.

But for the affiliate, 50% is a massive incentive. It turns them from a passive observer into an aggressive salesperson for your brand.

You are not "losing" 50%. You are paying a marketing fee only *after* the sale is made. It is risk-free advertising.

If you can get 100 affiliates to mail their lists on launch day, you don't have one sales team. You have an army.

**The Influencer Swarm: Manufactured Ubiquity**

One influencer posting about you is nice. It creates a blip.

Twenty influencers posting about you at the exact same hour is a **Signal**.

The human brain is wired to detect patterns. If a potential customer sees your product on Twitter, then sees it on Instagram, and then sees it in a YouTube video, all within 3 hours, they assume, *"This is the biggest thing in the world right now."*

This is a **Swarm.**

You don't need Kim Kardashian. She is too expensive and her audience is too broad.

You need **Micro-Influencers** (10k - 50k followers). They are hungry, affordable, and their audiences actually trust them.

**The Strategy:**

1. Identify 20 micro-influencers in your niche.
2. Pay them or give them equity/commission.
3. **The condition:** They must all post at **10:00 AM EST on Launch Day.**

You are artificially creating a "Trend." You are hacking the cultural conversation to make your breakout feel inevitable.

**The "Dream 100": The Gatekeepers**

The concept, popularized by Chet Holmes, is simple: 99% of people don't matter to your business. 1% do.

There are roughly 100 people in your industry who hold the keys to the kingdom. These are the podcasters, the bloggers, the thought leaders who command the attention of your entire market.

If *one* of them endorses you, you skip 2 years of "trust building."

You must stop marketing to the masses and start marketing to the **Gatekeepers**.

- Don't try to get 1,000 customers.
- Try to get **1** Gatekeeper who controls 1,000 customers.

This is not about spamming them. It is about **Relationship Asset Management.**

Send them free gifts. Share their content. Comment on their posts. Become valuable to *them* first.

When the Gatekeeper opens the gate, the flood follows.

**Actionable Takeaway: The "Win-Win" Pitch**

Most people pitch like beggars. "Please check out my book." "Please share my post."

Delete "Please" from your vocabulary.

You are offering them an asset, not asking for a favor.

Here is the template for the email you will send to your "Dream 100" and potential Affiliates.

**Subject: Partnership Idea For [Brand Name]**

**Body:**

*Hey [Name],*

*I've been following [Their Brand] for a while, loved your recent take on [Specific Topic].*

*I'm launching a new system called [Product Name] that helps your audience solve [Specific Pain Point] in 24 hours. It's exactly what your people are asking for.*

*I'm not asking for a shoutout. I want to partner.*

*I've set up a specialized link for you. You get **50% of every sale** that comes from your audience. My average cart value is $100, so you make $50 per click.*

*The launch is Tuesday. I've attached the product for free so you can see it's legit.*

*You in?*

*-[Your Name]*

**Why this works:**

1. **No fluff:** Respects their time.
2. **Specific compliment:** Proves you aren't a bot.
3. **The Number:** "50%" grabs their attention immediately.
4. **Zero Risk:** You gave them the product to vet.

Send this to 50 people. If 5 say yes, you are rich.

# Chapter 13: Outsourcing the Grind

**The Architect vs. The Bricklayer**

There is a disease in the entrepreneurial community called "Superman Syndrome."

It is the belief that because you *can* do something, you *should* do it.

"I can write the emails."

"I can design the logo."

"I can handle the customer support."

Yes, you can. And while you are doing those things, your bank account remains stagnant.

You are acting like a Bricklayer. The Bricklayer is noble, but he is paid by the hour, his back hurts, and he is easily replaced.

To achieve Hyper-Speed Wealth, you must be the **Architect**.

The Architect draws the blueprints. He looks at the skyline. He makes the high-level decisions. He never touches a trowel. He never mixes cement.

If you are spending your day doing work that can be done by a robot or a person earning $5 an hour, you are effectively paying yourself $5 an hour. You are the bottleneck of your own breakout.

You must fire yourself from the grind immediately.

**AI Staffing: The Infinite Intern**

In 2020, you needed $20,000 a month to hire a marketing team. You needed a Copywriter, a Graphic Designer, a Strategist, and a Coder.

Today, you need $20 a month.

Artificial Intelligence is not a "tool." It is **Digital Labor**.

- **ChatGPT / Claude:** This is your Copywriter and Strategist. It doesn't get writer's block. It doesn't ask for sick days. It writes 50 email variations in 10 seconds.
- **Mid journey / DALL-E:** This is your Graphic Designer. It creates logos, ad creatives, and website assets in 60 seconds that would take a human designer three days.

- **GitHub Copilot:** This is your Junior Developer. It writes the script to scrape data or build your landing page.

If you are writing your own blog posts from scratch, you are burning money.

If you are trying to learn Photoshop, you are burning money.

The new skill is not "doing the work." The new skill is **Prompt Engineering**, knowing how to command the digital army to do the work for you.

**Global Arbitrage: The $5 Genius**

Sometimes, AI isn't enough. You need human judgment. You need someone to pick up the phone, or manage a complex project, or show empathy.

Welcome to **Global Labor Arbitrage**.

We live in a global economy with local pricing.

The cost of living in New York City is 10x the cost of living in Manila or Bogota.

This means a "starvation wage" in New York is a "luxury wage" in the Philippines.

You can hire a university-educated, English-speaking, highly motivated executive assistant in the Philippines for $5 to $8 an hour.

They are not "cheap labor." They are **high-value talent** in a lower-cost geography.

If you are doing data entry, scheduling, or research, you are insulting your own potential.

Your job is to make $10,000 decisions.

Their job is to execute the $10 tasks that support those decisions.

This is not exploitation; it is economics. You provide a good job in their market; they provide time freedom in yours.

**Zapier: The Digital Nervous System**

If AI is the brain, and Global Talent is the hands, **Automation** is the nervous system.

You must build a machine that moves data without you touching it.

Tools like **Zapier** or **Make.com** act as the "glue" of the internet. They connect apps that don't normally talk to each other.

**The Old Way (Manual):**

1. Customer buys product on Stripe.
2. You copy their email.
3. You paste it into Mailchimp.
4. You send them a login link manually.
5. You add the sale to a Google Sheet for your accountant.

**The New Way (Automated):**

- **Trigger:** New Sale in Stripe.
- **Action 1:** Zapier adds email to Mailchimp.
- **Action 2:** Zapier sends Gmail with login details.
- **Action 3:** Zapier adds row to Google Sheets.
- **Action 4:** Zapier sends a "Ka-ching!" notification to your Slack channel.

Time elapsed: 0.1 seconds.

Human effort: Zero.

When you sleep, the machine works. When you are on a plane, the machine works.

A business that relies on your manual input is not a business; it is a toddler that needs constant babysitting.

**Actionable Takeaway: The "Zero-Human" Workflow Map**

Get a whiteboard or use a tool like Miro.

**Step 1: Map the Current Flow.**

Draw a box for every step in your business process, from "Stranger sees ad" to "Money in bank."

**Step 2: Identify the Human.**

Circle every box where *you* physically have to type, click, or talk.

- *Answering email inquiries?* (You)
- *Posting to Instagram?* (You)
- *Sending invoices?* (You)

**Step 3: The Replacement Strategy.**

Next to every circled box, write **AI**, **OUTSOURCE**, or **AUTOMATE**.

- *Writing Tweets* -> **AI** (ChatGPT generates them).
- *Posting Tweets* -> **AUTOMATE** (Type fully/ Hype fury schedules them).
- *Customer Support* -> **AI** (Chatbot) + **OUTSOURCE** (VA for complex issues).
- *Bookkeeping* -> **AUTOMATE** (Quick books integration).

**The Goal:**

Your map should eventually have zero circles around your name, except for one box at the very top: "**Strategy & Capital Allocation.**"

Everything else is the grind. And the grind is for the bricklayers.

# Chapter 14: The Tipping Point

## Pouring Gasoline on the Fire

There is a moment in every Midnight Breakout that is terrifying.

It isn't the moment of failure. You are used to failure. Failure is quiet. Failure is just an empty inbox and a silent phone.

The terrifying moment is when it **works.**

You wake up and you have 50 sales. The next hour, you have 100. Your phone is vibrating off the table. The server is groaning. People are emailing you demanding more.

This is the **Tipping Point.**

Most entrepreneurs misinterpret this signal. They panic. They think, "I can't handle this." They turn off the ads. They close the cart. They tap the brakes to "stabilize."

**Do not tap the brakes.**

When the fire starts, you do not reach for the water bucket. You reach for the gasoline.

The Tipping Point is the universe telling you that you have achieved **Product-Market Fit**. You are no longer pushing a boulder up a mountain; the boulder is rolling down the other side, and you are running for your life trying to keep up with it.

This is the moment where millionaires are made. If you hesitate here, you go back to being a turtle. If you commit here, you break the sound barrier.

## The Data Doesn't Lie

How do you know if you are truly at the Tipping Point or just having a lucky Tuesday?

You ignore your feelings. You look at the Dashboard.

There is one equation that matters more than anything else in business. It is the physics of wealth:

**LTV > CAC**

- **CAC (Cost to Acquire a Customer):** How much did you spend on ads/marketing to get one sale? (e.g., $20).
- **LTV (Lifetime Value):** How much profit does that customer give you over their life? (e.g., $100).

If you put 20 into the machine and it spits out 100, you do not have a business. You have a money printer.

If you have a money printer, what is the logical next step?

Do you print $100 and go to dinner?

No. You take every dollar you have, borrow every dollar you can find, and shove it into the machine until it breaks or runs out of paper.

- **The Trap:** If your CAC is $50 and your LTV is $50, you are just moving money around. Do not scale. You will just scale your bankruptcy.
- **The Green Light:** If your LTV is **3x** your CAC (e.g., Spend $30 to make $90), you have the Green Light.

## The Art of Doubling Down

Once the math proves the machine works, you must shift from "Experiment Mode" to "Aggression Mode."

This is where you violate the advice of your grandmothers.

Grandma says: "Debt is bad. Save your pennies."

The Breakout Author says: "Debt is leverage. Spend the pennies."

If you know, mathematically, that spending $1 makes you $3, then **speed is your only constraint.**

If you only reinvest your profits, you will grow linearly.

If you use **Leverage** (Credit Cards, Loans, Financing), you grow exponentially.

- **The Scenario:** You have a winning ad campaign. You are spending $1,000 a day. It is profitable.
- **The Move:** Raise the budget to $2,000 tomorrow. Then $5,000. Then $10,000.
- **The Fear:** "What if it stops working?"
- **The Reality:** It *will* stop working eventually. That is why you must extract maximum value *now*.

You maximize the credit line. You take the PayPal Working Capital loan. You pour every resource into the fire while the wind is blowing.

You can pay off the debt next month with the profits. But you cannot buy back the lost time if you let the fire die.

## The Point of No Return

The Tipping Point is a psychological barrier.

Before this moment, you were a "dabbler." You were "trying this out." You had a Plan B (your job, your savings).

When the metrics turn green, you must burn the boats.

You stop working on your other three side hustles. You stop looking for new ideas. You stop answering emails that aren't about *this* business.

You go **All In**.

This is the phase where you scale the team (Chapter 13), upgrade the servers (Chapter 10), and let the network know (Chapter 12).

You are riding a rogue wave. You cannot half-surf a rogue wave. You are either fully committed to riding it, or you will be crushed by it.

## Actionable Takeaway: The "Green Light" Metrics Sheet

Create a simple dashboard (Google Sheet or Excel). Update it every morning.

**The Traffic Light System:**

**RED LIGHT (Stop / Pivot):**

- **LTV:CAC Ratio:** Less than 1:1 (You are losing money).
- **Refund Rate:** > 10% (Your product is broken).
- **Conversion Rate:** < 0.5% (Your offer is weak).

**YELLOW LIGHT (Optimize / Wait):**

- **LTV:CAC Ratio:** 2:1 (You are making money, but margins are tight).
- **Churn:** 10-15% (You are losing customers too fast).
- **Traffic:** Inconsistent.

**GREEN LIGHT (GO GO GO):**

- **LTV:CAC Ratio: 3:1 or higher.** (Spend $1, make $3).
- **Payback Period:** < 30 Days. (You get your ad spend back fast).
- **NPS Score:** > 50 (Customers are raving).
- **Market Pull:** You have more demand than you can handle.

**The Rule:**

The second all lights turn **Green**, you empty the bank account into marketing. You do not sleep. You do not hesitate. You push the pedal to the floor until the engine screams.

# Chapter 15: The Adrenaline Crash

## The Empty Feeling of Winning

There is a dirty secret about getting rich that nobody tells you in the motivational YouTube videos.

They tell you about the champagne. They tell you about the freedom. They tell you about the pride.

They don't tell you about the **Crash**.

Imagine you are climbing Mount Everest. For years, your entire existence is defined by the climb. The struggle, the cold, the training, the adrenaline. You push through the pain because the Summit is everything.

Then, you reach the top. You plant the flag. You look around.

It takes about five minutes.

Then you realize: *It's just snow. It's cold. And now I have to go back down.*

The moment the wire transfer hits your account, that seven or eight-figure sum you spent your life dreaming about, you will not feel eternal bliss.

You will feel a spike of euphoria that lasts approximately 24 hours.

Then, you will feel a hollow, echoing emptiness.

You are the dog that finally caught the car. Now what?

## The Dopamine Withdrawal

To understand why winning feels like losing, you have to understand neurochemistry.

Dopamine is not the "Pleasure Molecule." That is a myth.

Dopamine is the **Pursuit Molecule**.

Nature designed you to hunt. When you are chasing the gazelle (or the deal, or the exit), your brain floods with dopamine to keep you moving. The anticipation of the reward is the high.

When you *get* the reward, the dopamine shuts off. Instantly.

You go from a biological high to a biological low. This is **Post-Success Depression**. It destroys lottery winners, gold medalists, and entrepreneurs alike.

You wake up the morning after the sale. The bank account is full, but the "Mission" is gone. You have no dragon to slay. You wander around your house feeling directionless, irritable, and bored.

If you are not prepared for this crash, you will try to fix it with destructive behavior. You will start gambling, taking drugs, or starting a new, risky business just to feel the "chase" again.

Recognize the crash for what it is: A chemical reset. Do not fight it. Do not try to medicate it. Just sit in the quiet.

## The Lamborghini Trap (Lifestyle Creep)

The most dangerous person is a poor person who suddenly becomes rich.

They have spent their lives in scarcity. Now, facing abundance, they have an uncontrollable urge to "prove" they made it.

This is **Lifestyle Creep**.

You see the number in the bank. You think, "I can afford the Lamborghini. I can afford the penthouse. I can afford the $20,000 watch."

Mathematically? Yes, you can buy it.

Strategically? You are putting the handcuffs back on.

Wealth is not the car you drive. **Wealth is the money you have not spent.**

The moment you trade your cash for a liability (a car that depreciates), you are deleting your freedom.

If you make $2 million and immediately spend $500,000 on toys, you have signaled to the world that you are "rich," but you have just reduced your survivability by 25%.

The goal of the Midnight Breakout was to escape the rat race. If you buy a lifestyle that requires $50,000 a month to maintain, **you just built**

**a new, more expensive rat race.** You have to keep working to feed the beast.

Stay in the cheap apartment for six months. Keep the old car. Let the money sit there. Let it harden into concrete before you start chipping away at it.

## Imposter Syndrome: "I Got Lucky"

In the quiet days following the windfall, a voice will whisper in your ear.

*"You didn't earn this. You just got lucky. You were in the right place at the right time. You are a fraud."*

This is **Imposter Syndrome**.

And here is the truth: **The voice is partially right.**

You *did* get lucky.

The market timing was luck. The viral algorithm was luck. The buyer's mood was luck.

But remember Chapter 4 (The Sniper) and Chapter 2 (Asymmetry).

You **engineered** the luck.

Thousands of people saw the same market trends you did. They did nothing.

Thousands of people had the same tools. They watched Netflix.

You stood in the rain with the bucket. You built the trap. You took the asymmetric bet.

Luck is a lightning strike. But you built the lightning rod.

Do not apologize for your success. But do not get arrogant, either. Acknowledge that the universe gave you a push, and your job now is to steward that gift, not squander it.

## Actionable Takeaway: The 30-Day "No Splurge" Contract

You are biologically compromised right now. Your brain is swimming in chemicals. You are not fit to make financial decisions.

You need a cooling-off period.

**The Contract:**

Print this out. Sign it. Tape it to your mirror.

***I, [Name], having recently achieved a financial breakout, hereby agree to the following terms for the next 30 DAYS:***

1. ***The Freeze: I will not make any single purchase over $500 that is not a recurring utility (rent/food).***
2. ***No Big Toys: I will not buy a car, a house, a watch, or a vacation.***
3. ***No "Angel" Investing: I will not give money to friends, family, or "great business ideas" pitched to me. I will say, "My accountant has frozen my funds for tax audits."***
4. ***The Lockbox: I will move 80% of the cash into a separate, high-yield savings account that is annoying to access.***
5. ***The Silence: I will not post about my wealth on social media.***

***Signed:*** ______________________________

***Date:*** _________________

Survive the crash. Secure the bag. The celebration can wait 30 days.

# Chapter 16: The Moat

## From Flash Cash to Fortress

You have done the impossible. You broke out. You have a number in your bank account that looks like a phone number.

Now, you are in the most dangerous position of your life.

Making money requires being an aggressor. It requires risk, speed, and concentration.

*Keeping* money requires the exact opposite. It requires paranoia, patience, and diversification.

If you keep acting like a cowboy after you have won the rodeo, you will get trampled. We have all seen the headlines: The pro athlete who makes $100 million and goes bankrupt in five years. The lottery winner who is back in the trailer park in two.

They had the Castle (the money), but they didn't dig the **Moat**.

The Moat is the defensive structure that separates you from poverty. Without it, the barbarians, inflation, lawsuits, bad decisions, and market crashes, will storm the gates and take everything back.

## Liquidity is Not Wealth

The first thing you must understand is that **Cash is Trash.**

This hurts to hear. You just worked so hard to get the cash. It feels good to look at the balance. It feels safe.

It is a lie.

Fiat currency (Dollars, Euros, Yen) is designed to lose value. It is an ice cube melting in the sun. If inflation is 5% (and it is likely higher), your million dollars is becoming $950,000 in purchasing power every year just by sitting there.

If you leave your wealth in cash, you are bleeding to death slowly.

**Flash Cash**, the money you made from a crypto spike, a product launch, or an exit, is volatile. It is "New Money." It is flighty.

**Old Money** is heavy. It is grounded in things that are hard to destroy.

Your mission in this chapter is to convert your ephemeral, melting digital numbers into hard, boring, physical reality.

## The Boring Bucket

How do you dig the Moat? You become incredibly, painfully boring.

To *get* rich, you concentrated your bets (you went all-in on your business/idea).

To *stay* rich, you must diversify.

You need to move your Flash Cash into the **Boring Bucket**.

**1. Real Estate:**

Land. Apartment buildings. Commercial warehouses. God is not making any more land. Real estate is illiquid (hard to sell), which is actually a feature, not a bug. It prevents you from panic-selling when you get scared. It pays you rent while you sleep.

**2. Broad Market Index Funds:**

Do not pick stocks. You are not Warren Buffett. Buy the entire S&P 500 or the Total World Stock Market. You are betting on human civilization. If the top 500 companies in the world go to zero, your money won't matter anyway because we will be hunting squirrels for food.

**3. Gold/Hard Assets:**

A small percentage in things that governments cannot print. This is your insurance policy against the world going crazy.

**The Rule:** If your investments are exciting, you are gambling. Your Moat should be so boring that you forget to check it.

## Never Go Back

The ultimate nightmare is not losing the money. The ultimate nightmare is having to go back to the cubicle.

The purpose of the Moat is to ensure you never have to trade time for money again.

We call this **Financial Escape Velocity.**

If you have 2,000,000 in your Boring Bucket, and it yields a conservative 80,000 a year in passive income.

Can you live on $80,000?

If yes, you are free. You never *have* to work again. You can work because you *want* to (which is a totally different feeling).

If you blow the principal on a Lamborghini and your nest egg drops to $500k, your passive income drops to $20,000. Now you can't survive. Now you have to go back to the boss and beg for a job.

That is a fate worse than death. Protect the principal at all costs.

## Actionable Takeaway: The "Waterfall" System

Do not trust your willpower to manage your windfall. Build a system that manages it for you. This is the **Waterfall.**

Imagine your income (the big exit check or the monthly launch revenue) hitting a series of buckets at the top of a waterfall. It fills the first, spills over to the second, and so on.

**Bucket 1: The Tax Vault (30-40%)**

- **Priority:** Critical.
- Before you spend a dime, move the government's cut to a separate account. Do not touch this. The IRS has guns. You do not want to fight them.

**Bucket 2: The Emergency Dam (6 Months Expenses)**

- **Priority:** High.
- Keep 6 months of living expenses in cash. This is for peace of mind. If the car breaks or the roof leaks, you don't have to sell an asset.

**Bucket 3: The Moat (50% of what remains)**

- **Priority:** High.
- This money flows immediately into your boring assets (Vanguard ETFs, Real Estate down payments). This money is gone. Pretend it doesn't exist. This is your Freedom Fund.

**Bucket 4: The Play Fund (What's left)**

- **Priority:** Low.
- This is for the nice watch, the trip, or the risky crypto bet. If you blow this, it doesn't matter, because your Tax, Safety, and Freedom buckets are full.

**The Assignment:**

Log into your bank account right now. Open three sub-accounts: **TAX**, **MOAT**, and **PLAY**.

Set up automatic transfers.

Be the Architect of your own defense.

# Chapter 17: Tax Warfare

## It's Not What You Make; It's What You Keep

There is a silent partner in your business.

He does not wake up at 4 AM. He does not take risks. He does not code. He does not handle customer support. He adds zero value to the enterprise.

Yet, the moment you succeed, he kicks down your door and demands 40% to 50% of the loot.

His name is Uncle Sam (or the Crown, or the State, depending on where you sleep).

Most people view taxes as a "civil duty" or an "unavoidable tragedy." They make a million dollars, write a check for $450,000 to the IRS, and pat themselves on the back for being good citizens.

This is the mindset of a serf.

The wealthy view taxes differently. To the wealthy, the Tax Code is not a law book; it is a **Rule Book**. It is a game of strategy.

If you make $1 million and keep $600,000, you have lost the game.

If you make $1 million and keep $950,000, you have mastered the game.

You are engaged in **Tax Warfare**. Your enemy is bureaucracy. Your weapon is the law. If you do not fight, you are volunteering to be robbed.

*(Disclaimer: I am an author, not a CPA or an attorney. This is high-level strategy, not legal advice. Hire a professional, which is the entire point of this chapter.)*

## The Historian vs. The Shark

The single biggest mistake new millionaires make is keeping their old accountant.

Your family accountant, "Nice Guy Dave," who has filed your W-2 tax returns for ten years, is useless to you now. Dave is a **Historian**.

He looks at the past. You hand him a shoebox of receipts in April, he records what happened, puts the numbers in the boxes, and tells you what you owe.

He is reactive. He is terrified of an audit. His goal is to file the return and go play golf.

You do not need a Historian. You need a **Shark**.

A Shark (a High-Net-Worth Tax Strategist) looks at the *future.*

He calls you in November, before the year ends, and says: *"You made too much money this month. Go buy a G-Wagon. Pre-pay your marketing for next year. Move $50,000 into a defined benefit plan. If we don't move this money by December 31st, you lose $100,000."*

The Historian costs $500 a year and costs you millions in lost opportunities.

The Shark costs $10,000 a year and saves you hundreds of thousands.

The Shark is an investment with an ROI higher than Bitcoin. Find him. Hire him.

## The Entity Shield

If you are operating as a Sole Proprietor, you are walking through a battlefield naked.

The tax code was written by business owners, for business owners. Employees (W-2) get taxed on the *first* dollar they earn. Business owners get taxed on the *last* dollar they earn (after expenses).

You must wrap yourself in the armor of **Entities**.

1. **The LLC / S-Corp (The Shield):**
   This allows you to split your income. You pay yourself a "reasonable salary" (subject to expensive payroll taxes) and take the rest as a "distribution" (not subject to self-employment taxes).
   - *The Math:* On $1 million profit, this simple switch can save you $20,000+ instantly.

2. **The Trust (The Ghost):**
   "Own nothing, control everything."
   Rockefeller lived by this. If you get sued, and you own the assets personally, you lose. If a Trust owns the assets, and you are just the beneficiary, the assets are often untouchable. Trusts also solve the estate tax problem, ensuring your dynasty doesn't get cut in half when you die.

## Location Independence: The Nuclear Option

If you hit a massive Midnight Breakout, let's say an exit of $5 million or $10 million, where you sleep becomes a multi-million dollar decision.

We live in a remote world. You can run your digital empire from anywhere. So why run it from a jurisdiction that hates you?

This is **Geo-Arbitrage**.

1. **State Level (USA):**
   Moving from California (13.3% state tax) or New York to Texas, Florida, or Nevada (0% state tax) is an instant 13% raise. On a 10M exit, that is 1.3 million in your pocket just for buying a plane ticket.
2. **Act 60 (Puerto Rico):**
   The ultimate loophole for Americans. You move to Puerto Rico. You spend 183 days a year there. Your federal tax rate drops from 37% to **4%**. Your capital gains tax drops to **0%**. You keep your US Passport. You keep your citizenship. You just opt out of the IRS looting.

**Note;** For my international readers, look for your region's equivalent of a Tax Haven (e.g., Dubai, Portugal's NHR, etc.).

1. **International (Dubai / Caymans):**
   If you are willing to leave your home country fully, places like Dubai offer **0% income tax**. You make $10 million; you keep

$10 million.

If you stay in a high-tax zone out of "loyalty" or laziness, realize that you are paying a subscription fee of millions of dollars for the privilege of bad weather and potholes.

## Actionable Takeaway: The Shark Interview

You are going to fire "Nice Guy Dave" this week. You are going to interview three new CPA firms.

Here are the questions you ask to determine if they are Sharks or Historians.

**1. "How often will we communicate?"**

- *Bad Answer:* "Once a year during tax season." (Fire them).
- *Good Answer:* "Quarterly strategy calls to adjust for your income."

**2. "Where on the scale of 1 to 10 are you regarding aggressiveness?"**

- *Bad Answer:* "We prefer to be conservative to avoid audits." (Cowardice).
- *Good Answer:* "We follow the letter of the law, but we interpret the gray areas in your favor. We aim for a 9."

**3. "What do you think about [Real Estate Depreciation / Cost Segregation / R&D Credits]?"**

- *Bad Answer:* "Those are complicated/risky." (Incompetence).
- *Good Answer:* "We use those standardly for clients with your income profile."

**4. "Do you invest your own money?"**

- *Bad Answer:* "No, I just save."
- *Good Answer:* "Yes, I own real estate and businesses." (You want an accountant who understands wealth, not just tax forms).

**The Rule:** If your accountant doesn't make you slightly nervous, you are overpaying your taxes. Get a Shark.

# Chapter 18: The Next Morning

## Resetting the Scoreboard to Zero

So, you did it.

You followed the blueprint. You built the trap. You caught the asymmetric bet. You survived the crash. You dug the moat.

You wake up on a Tuesday morning. The sun is shining. The coffee smells the same. Your dog still needs to go out.

But when you open your banking app, the number is different. It has two commas. Maybe three.

You are free. You never have to work again. You have achieved the "Midnight Breakout."

Now, I have to tell you the hardest truth in this entire book. The truth that, if I had told you in Chapter 1, you would have thrown this book in the trash.

**The money didn't fix you.**

If you were anxious poor, you are now anxious rich.

If you were lonely poor, you are now lonely rich.

If you were insecure poor, you are now insecure rich, and paranoid that people only like you for your money.

The Breakout solves your *survival* problems. It deletes the stress of rent, food, and bills.

But it does not solve your *existential* problems. In fact, it magnifies them.

Now that the noise of "survival" is gone, the silence of "purpose" is deafening.

## The "Number" Fallacy

We all suffer from the "Number" Fallacy.

*"When I hit $1 million, I will be happy."*

*"When I hit $10 million, I will feel successful."*

This is a mirage. The horizon moves as you approach it.

If you have $1 million, you hang out with people who have $10 million. You feel poor.

If you have $10 million, you hang out with people who have private jets. You feel poor.

Money is a tool, not a cure. It is like gasoline. Gasoline is essential to move the car. But if you fill the tank and you don't have a destination, you are just sitting in a driveway inhaling fumes.

You have spent your entire life climbing the ladder. Now you are at the top.

Make sure the ladder is leaning against the right wall.

## From Mercenary to Missionary

During the Breakout phase (Chapters 1-14), you were a **Mercenary**.

A Mercenary fights for money. He asks, "What is the ROI?" "How can I flip this?" "Where is the arbitrage?"

There is no shame in being a Mercenary. When you are broke, you *must* be a Mercenary. You need to buy your freedom.

But a Mercenary who keeps fighting after he has won the war becomes a psychopath.

Once the money is secured, you must transition to being a **Missionary**.

A Missionary fights for a cause. A Missionary asks, "What is the impact?" "What is the legacy?" "How does this help?"

- **Mercenary:** "How can I sell more plastic widgets to get rich?"
- **Missionary:** "How can I clean the plastic out of the ocean?"

Ironically, the Missionary often makes *more* money than the Mercenary because people want to follow him. But the motivation is different.

If you stay a Mercenary forever, you will die with a full bank account and an empty funeral.

## Zeroing Out

The greatest danger to your wealth is not the market; it is your own ego.

Success makes you soft. It makes you think you are a genius. It makes you lazy.

To sustain the Midnight Breakout, you must practice the art of **Zeroing Out**.

Every morning, when you wake up, you must mentally reset the scoreboard to 0-0.

The money in the bank? That's for Defense (The Moat). It doesn't count for today's game.

Yesterday's home run does not win today's game.

Look at the greats. Kobe Bryant didn't look at his rings and skip practice. He trained harder than the rookies.

Why? Because he wasn't playing for the money anymore. He was playing for **Mastery**.

If you start thinking, "I made it," you are finished. The market will devour you.

You must wake up with the same hunger you had when you were broke, not because you *need* the money, but because you *respect* the game.

## The Real Breakout

This book was titled *"The Midnight Breakout."*

You thought it meant breaking out of poverty.

And it did.

But the *real* breakout is breaking out of the matrix of external validation.

It is realizing that you don't need the Lambo to impress people you don't like.

It is realizing that time is more valuable than digits on a screen.

It is realizing that the ultimate luxury is not a gold watch; it is the ability to sit quietly in a room and create something beautiful without asking for permission.

You have the money. You have the tools. You have the freedom.

Now, for the first time in your life, the choice is actually yours.

Don't screw it up.

## Actionable Takeaway: The Post-Wealth Bucket List

Most people have a bucket list of things to buy (Houses, Cars, Boats). That is the "Pre-Wealth" list. You can buy those now. They are boring.

I want you to write your **Post-Wealth Bucket List.**

These are the things that **cannot be bought**. These are the things that require effort, pain, and time, regardless of your net worth.

**The Rules:**

1. You cannot write a check to achieve it.
2. It must improve your character, body, or relationships.

**Examples:**

- *Get six-pack abs.* (You can't buy this. You have to sweat).
- *Learn to speak fluent Japanese.* (You can't buy this. You have to study).
- *Raise kind children who don't act like spoiled brats.* (You can't buy this. You have to parent).
- *Read 50 books a year.*
- *Master the piano.*

Write down five items.

This is your new job. This is your new mountain.

The money is just the hiking boots. Now, start climbing.

www.ingramcontent.com/pod-product-compliance
Lightning Source LLC
LaVergne TN
LVHW090427210926
848480LV00002B/720

* 9 7 9 8 2 3 3 6 5 0 5 6 7 *